GEOMETRIC PATCHWORK PATTERNS

FULL-SIZE CUT-OUTS AND INSTRUCTIONS FOR 12 QUILTS

CAROL BELANGER GRAFTON

DOVER PUBLICATIONS, INC., NEW YORK

Published in Canada by General Publishing Company Ltd., 30 Lesmill Road, Don Mills, Toronto,
Ontario.
Published in the United Kingdom by Constable
and Company, Ltd., 10 Orange Street, London WC 2.

Geometric Patchwork Patterns is a new work,
first published by Dover Publications, Inc., in 1975.

International Standard Book Number: 0-486-23183-6
Library of Congress Catalog Card Number: 74-31894

Manufactured in the United States of America
Dover Publications, Inc.
180 Varick Street
New York, N.Y. 10014

INTRODUCTION

The twelve patchwork patterns in this book are among the most beautiful to behold as well as the most exciting to work. The crisp, angular preciseness that they all feature is a perfect foil for the warm, colorful, homespun-looking fabrics so popular with quilt makers. Probably the main reason these patterns have always been popular is that they lend themselves so well to personal adaptation—particularly in regard to the color scheme to be used. To a greater degree than with more representational motifs—such as pineapples, schoolhouses, trees, etc.—geometric designs have a way of changing dramatically with different color schemes. Thus our color specifications are mere suggestions, and you should feel free to make them more or less complicated and more or less subtle in order to achieve quilts that are your personal creations.

These patterns selected for this collection provide challenges to both beginners and experts. Even more than the novices, those who have already made quilts by copying out designs onto cardboard will appreciate the convenience of the unusual feature of this collection—the carefully designed preprinted cardboard patterns or templates that make up the last half of this publication.

As the title indicates, this work is a collection of immediately useable patterns—not an instruction book on how to do patchwork; that subject is already well covered in numerous inexpensive books (one of the best of which is *The Standard Book of Quilt Making and Collecting* by Marguerite Ickis[1]), and limitations of space permit us only to sketch out the process in brief.

---

[1]A Dover paperback reprint (0-486-20582-7, 280pp., $3.50.

BEGINNING THE QUILT

Kinds of Materials

At the beginning of each pattern, we indicate the amount of 36-inch-wide material you will need to complete a quilt of the specified dimensions. Of course, you are free to revise both the color scheme and the proposed finished size of the quilt; the latter adjustment is accomplished by adding additional blocks or half-blocks to both the width and height, and then adjusting the length of the four border pieces.

The first rule to observe in selecting material for a quilt is to combine the same kinds of fabrics. For instance, linens and cottons go together, silks and satins, and so on. If you want to make a quilt that can be laundered, be sure that *all* the material used is washable and pre-shrunk and that the colors are fast.

For your convenience in sewing, select a soft material, not too closely woven. Closely woven cloth makes the needlework more difficult and is no stronger than thinner goods. Materials that are stiff because of being "treated" with a finish are also difficult to work with. In general, the following materials are good for patchwork quilts: gingham, percale, calico, shirting, broadcloth, and cotton-polyester blends.

Cutting Out the Pattern Pieces

What could be simpler than to cut the pattern pieces carefully on the dashed lines? Note that these pattern pieces take into consideration the 1/4" seam allowance that is so necessary to patchwork. It is important to keep the edges of the cardboard as neat and firm as possible, so use very sharp, good-sized scissors, a single-edged razor blade or an X-acto knife. Some people prefer to cut out all the pattern pieces pertaining to the design at one time, but novices often cut them out one at a time and then cut the appropriate amount of fabric for each one before working with the next pattern piece.

Cutting the Fabric

Cutting is one of the most important steps in making your quilt. You must be accurate in order to have the pattern fit perfectly and to avoid wasting your materials. Have sharp scissors with blades at least 4 inches long. You will need a ruler for marking straight lines, and a pencil with hard lead to avoid blurry marks around the pattern. With these tools at hand, proceed as follows:

1. Press all materials perfectly smooth to eliminate wrinkles.

2. Take one of the cardboard pieces—say Piece No. 1—and refer to the preliminary instructions for the design to find out how many pieces of each fabric you need to complete the quilt. You may want to jot this information down in pencil on the pattern piece itself; i.e., 48 P[ink], 48 G[reen], etc.

3. Next lay one of the cardboard patterns near the top left edge of the material (but not on the selvage), making sure that the long part of the pattern runs parallel with the straight grain of the fabric. Trace around the cardboard with a hard lead pencil.

4. Continue moving the cardboard pattern and tracing it on the fabric the required number of times, moving from left to right, always keeping the long part of the pattern running with the straight grain. Allow a little space between tracings, to make it easier to cut the pieces out.

5. After you have traced the first pattern piece the required number of times, take one of the other pattern pieces that is to be cut from the same material and trace it in a similar manner, again referring to the preliminary instructions to find out the required number of pieces.

6. Carefully cut out the required number of pieces of each color and then organize them according to shape and color. Most people find it convenient to string

them together with a single thread running through the center of each (see Figure 1).

7. Even though the fabric requirements have been very carefully calculated it is still a good idea to cut out all the pieces for the entire quilt before one begins to sew, just to make absolutely certain that you have enough material of each color.

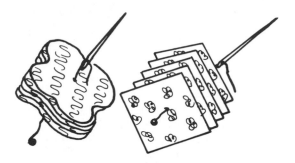

Figure 1 STRINGING PATCHES TOGETHER
Run thread through center of patches according to shape and color. Knot at bottom and lift off patch from top as needed.

Marking Seam Allowance

There are at least two accurate methods of marking the 1/4" seam allowance that is so necessary to fitting the pattern pieces together to form blocks.

1. Using a dressmaker's hem gauge or a ruler, with a pencil mark the seam allowance on the fabric.

2. Since most fabrics used in quilting are lightweight and semi-transparent, it is often possible to put the cut pieces over the corresponding template and "read" the seam allowance indication, tracing it in pencil on the fabric itself.

Sewing

The simple stitches employed in quilt making are the running stitch (used in piecing parts of the design together and also in quilt stitching) and the hemming stitch (used in appliqué work). See Figure 2.

Use No. 60 thread and a short needle, No. 8. A long needle is not necessary, for very few stitches are taken before drawing the needle

Figure 2 RUNNING STITCH
Begin at right, sewing toward left. Knot of thread is on under side of material. In quilting, take stitches about 1/16 inch and space evenly.

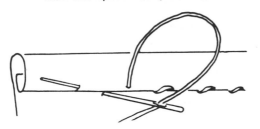

HEMMING STITCH
Sewing from right to left, the needle catches folded edge of hem to the material. Spacing varies according to material.

through the material. Use white thread unless the patches are cut from very dark cloth. Sew patches together to form blocks, referring to the block diagram that accompanies the preliminary instructions. Use small running stitches to secure each short seam, and then finish with at least two back stitches. The seam should be ¼" wide and sewn as straight as possible.

Work each block individually and sew several patches together at a time to form a small section of it. Fit sections together to see that the adjoining parts fit exactly. In order to have it perfectly correct, tack corners together with a few over-stitches. Sew the sections together with the usual ¼" seam.

After you have pieced the block, press it on the wrong side with a warm iron. Press the seams flat—not open.

As for using a sewing machine, old-time quilters frown on anything but the finest hand-sewing when piecing blocks. However, the sewing machine can serve a useful purpose when you are ready to set the blocks together —more about this below.

Setting the Quilt

After you have pieced the required number of blocks, lay them out to get the final effect before setting them together. Check to make sure that each block is turned the proper way,

and that the border, if you are using one, fits precisely. As you survey the blocks, keep in mind that they are not yet sewn together and that the seams, when they are finished, will each account for taking up ¼"; of course, this affects the fitting of the border, both as to length and width.

You can now proceed with setting the blocks together. The best way is to join all the blocks of one row, sewing them with a ¼" seam. Continue joining blocks one row at a time. Some people feel that machine sewing here not only saves time but also strengthens the long seams. Others believe that it is easier to keep the pattern accurate and the corners matched if the work is done by hand. Some hand-sewers also find that the close machine stitches create difficulties later on when one gets ready to do the final quilt stitching.

In sewing on the border strips, begin with the shorter pieces of the top and bottom first. Baste them before stitching. Then handle the side border pieces the same way.

Blocking the Quilt

The term "blocking" means keeping the edges straight on all sides of the quilt so that it will be a perfect rectangle when finished. The term applies to the quilt's divisions and blocks, and also to the border, so the process of blocking is a continuing process from start to finish.

Right at the start, it will help your blocking if you have cut the pieces and blocks according to the warp and weft threads in the material, as we discussed it in the section on Cutting the Fabric. Observance of this rule eliminates the tendency to pucker.

Pull the edges of the block straight with the fingers and pin the corners to the ironing board to hold them rigidly in place. Cover the block with a damp cloth and steam with a warm iron. Do not let the pressing cloth get dry. Press the edges until they are perfectly straight and of equal measurements. The center is pressed last.

It is a good idea to press each block after the sewing is completed. This is also true of the border sections. This means quite a lot of pressing, but it assures greater accuracy in the final measurements of all units. After the quilt is set together, it will need a final blocking before it is ready to be quilted to the filling and lining.

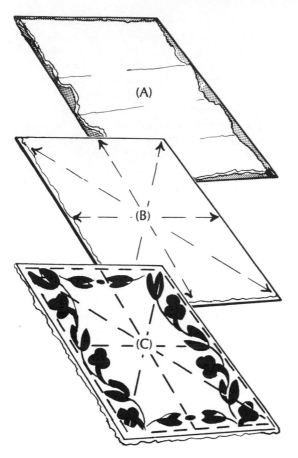

Figure 3 BASTING PROCEDURE
(A) *Placing cotton batting on lining.*
(B) *Basting cotton batting to lining.*
(C) *Basting top to batting and lining, through center and around edges.*

FINISHING THE QUILT

Quilt Filling and Lining

You should choose the filling for your quilt with the greatest care if you want it to endure for years. It is false economy to use inferior cotton or wool which has not been properly treated. Your time and painstaking stitching deserve the best material. You may obtain cotton batting that is especially prepared for quilt filling. It comes in large sheets carefully folded and rolled. Perhaps you will need two packages, depending on the size of the quilt.

The back of the quilt is made of lengths of soft material sewn together for correct width and length. It should be soft and loosely woven to make the quilt stitching easier. The over-all measurements should be 2 inches longer on each side to allow for binding when the quilt

is completed. Carefully arrange the lining on a large flat surface, and fasten the corners with thumb tacks. Unroll the cotton batting and spread it out evenly on the lining, making sure there are no lumps or thin places that will make the quilting uneven.

Next, fasten the cotton batting securely to the lining with long basting stitches. Start in the center of the quilt, and sew toward the edge until you have a number of diagonal lines, as shown in Figure 3. You are now ready to lay the neatly pressed top in place over the lining and the cotton filling. Smooth it out and see that the edges correspond on all four sides. The three layers are now basted together just as you basted the first two—in diagonal lines from the center to the edges of the quilt.

The Quilting Stitch

The actual quilt stitching is a simple process for any one who can do any other form of needlework, but it does take a little practice. The first attempt should be in stitching straight lines, with curves and feathers coming later. It is helpful to use a practice piece of two squares of material with a layer of cotton in between. Try stitching the pieces together with a plain running stitch. You will soon learn the best method of pushing the needle in and out, and also the direction in which to sew. You will be sure to find that it is easier to sew *toward* you.

It is an interesting fact that many busy women who enjoy piecing blocks, but who do not care for the final quilting of the three layers, procure the services of professional quilters. There are church organizations, craft shops and private seamstresses who accept quilting at fair rates.

One reason why quilt stitching is often "farmed out" is that it is greatly simplied when done on a quiting frame, which is cumbersome. However, quilting can also be done successfully, if less rapidly, on a quilting hoop.

The purpose of the quilting stitch is to firmly lock the top of the quilt to both its filling and lining. In primitive times, the three layers were held together by stitches at only a few main points, called the counter points or quilt points. Next came interlacing diagonal lines, forming squares and diamonds, then quilt stitching gradually developed into more elaborate designs having a central motif and a border with a "fill-in" space between.

Quilt stitching is used in all kinds of quilts —comforter, appliquéd and patchwork. When the quilt is composed of squares, the quilting stitches cover the plain squares which alternate with the decorated ones, and this gives the effect of throwing the decorated part into more pronounced relief. These quilting stitches in the plain squares are sometimes in straight or diagonal lines and are usually planned to form a contrast to the appliquéd or pieced blocks. Thus, straight lines are chosen to contrast with a curving design, and curves and whirls are chosen when the main pattern is straight or geometrical.

A few popular quilting designs are shown in Figure 4. The pattern that is chosen is traced on the quilt top in chalk in dark-colored areas and in lead pencil in light-colored ones. Use a short Sharp needle, size No. 8-9. The choice of thread should be between Nos. 50 and 70, preferably white. It is important to start the quilting near the center of the frame because it is always easier to sew toward the body. To commence, make a knot at the end of the thread and bring the needle through to the top of the quilt, then pull gently but firmly and the knot will slip through the lower layer into the padding where it will not be seen. To finish off, make a single back stitch and run the thread through the padding. Cut, and the end will be lost.

Figure 4 TYPICAL QUILTING DESIGNS
(A) *All-over patterns.*
(B) *Patterns for narrow strips and borders.*

Binding the Quilt

When the quilting is completed, trim the edges (except the lining extension if used for binding) on all four sides in an even line, being sure to remove any cotton that extends beyond the quilt's top. There are two methods for binding the edges: (1) Make use of the 2-inch extension of the back lining which was left on during the quilting process. Even it off all around, turn up an edge for a seam, and fold up over the top of the quilt. Sew in place with small hemming stitches in matching color thread. (2) Bind the edges with bias strips, if you are going to use a binding of different color or a scalloped border. Cut the bias strips 1 inch wide and sew them together. The binding is done by laying the bias strip along the outside edge of the quilt, and fitting the edges together so they match exactly. Sew the bias strip and all three layers together with a ¼-inch seam, using a running stitch. After the sewing is done, turn the quilt over and turn down the edges of the bias strip ¼ inch. Fold this over the back of the quilt and sew securely to the bottom layer with small hemming stitches.

DOUBLE "Z" QUILT

SIZE OF QUILT

This quilt, measuring 78 x 96 inches, is made up of eighty 9–inch pieced blocks set eight in width and ten in length with a 3–inch plain border.

NUMBER OF PIECES TO BE CUT

NOTE: Cut strips first to get full length without piecing.

Piece No. 1 . . . . .320 White
Piece No. 2 . . . . .480 White
Piece No. 2 . . . . .160 Dark Color
Piece No. 2 . . . . .160 Light Color
Piece No. 3 . . . . .160 Dark Color
Piece No. 3 . . . . .160 Light Color

2 strips, 3½ x 78½ inches . . White
2 strips, 3½ x 96½ inches . . White

AMOUNT OF MATERIAL

White . . . . .7 yards
Dark Color . . . . . .2½ yards
Light Color . . . . . .2½ yards

COLOR CHART

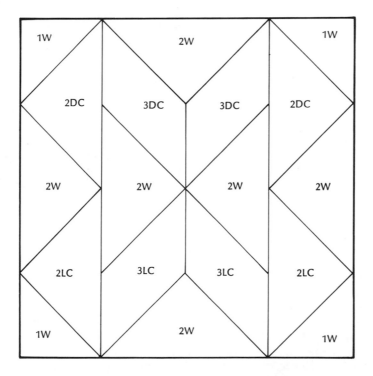

LEGEND

W — White
LC — Light Color
DC — Dark Color

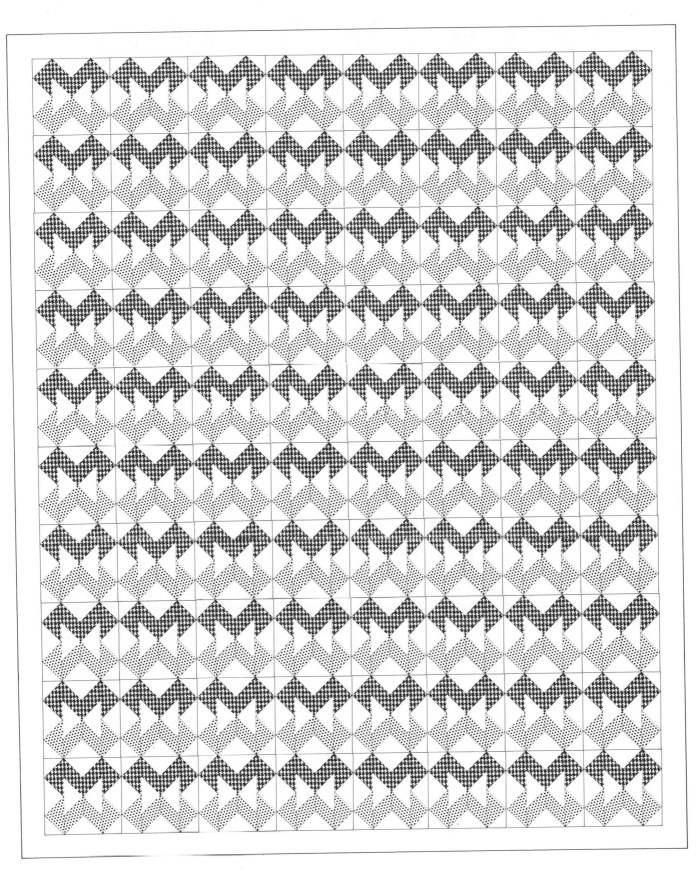

Patterns for this quilt are given on page 33.

STONE MASON'S PUZZLE QUILT

SIZE OF QUILT

This quilt, measuring 81 x 99 inches, is made up of ninety-nine 9–inch pieced blocks set nine in width and eleven in length.

NUMBER OF PIECES TO BE CUT

Piece No. 1.................. 99 White
Piece No. 1..................396 Green
Piece No. 2..................396 White
Piece No. 3..................792 White
Piece No. 4..................792 Green

AMOUNT OF MATERIAL

White ....6¾ yards
Green ....6¼ yards

COLOR CHART

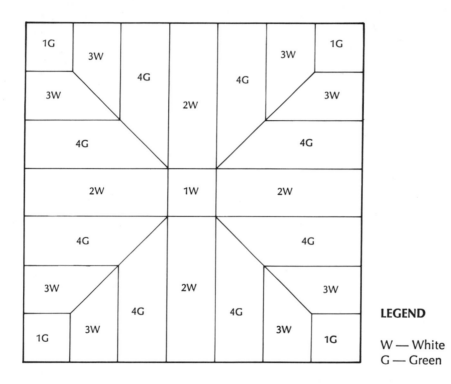

LEGEND

W — White
G — Green

Patterns for this quilt are given on page 33.

BRUNSWICK STAR QUILT

SIZE OF QUILT

This quilt, measuring 84 x 102 inches, is made up of twenty 18–inch pieced blocks set four in width and five in length with a 6–inch plain border.

NUMBER OF PIECES TO BE CUT

NOTE: Cut strips first to get full length without piecing.

Piece No. 1 . . . . 40 White
Piece No. 2 . . . . 60 Light Blue
Piece No. 2 . . . . 60 Dark Blue
Piece No. 2 . . . . .120 White
Piece No. 3 . . . . 80 White
Piece No. 4 . . . . .120 Red

2 strips 6½ x 84½ inches . . . . Light Blue
2 strips 6½ x 104 inches . . . . . Light Blue

AMOUNT OF MATERIAL

White . . . . .4¾ yards
Red . . . . .3 yards
Light Blue . . . . . . .3¼ yards
Dark Blue . . . . . . .1 yard

COLOR CHART

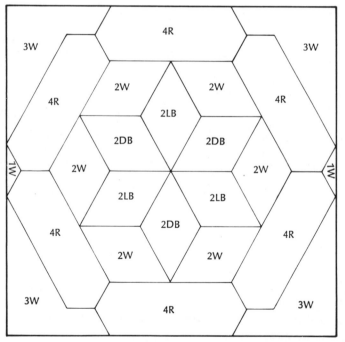

LEGEND

W — White
R — Red
LB — Light Blue
DB — Dark Blue

Patterns for this quilt are given on page 35.

THE COLUMBIA QUILT

SIZE OF QUILT

This quilt, measuring 78 x 99 inches, is made up of a continuous pattern, rather than pieced blocks. You can easily vary the size of the quilt by adding a row of stars to or subtracting a row of stars from the length or width.

NUMBER OF PIECES TO BE CUT

Piece No. 1............252 Light Blue
Piece No. 1............252 Dark Blue
Piece No. 1............252 Print
Piece No. 2............138 White
Piece No. 2a........... 24 White*
Piece No. 2b........... 10 White†
Piece No. 3............ 12 White§
Piece No. 4............ 4 White‡

*Piece No. 2a is used *only* along the side edges of the quilt.
†Piece No. 2b is used *only* along the top and bottom edges of the quilt.
§Piece No. 3 is used *only* along the top and bottom edges of the quilt.
‡Piece No. 4 is used *only* at the four corners of the quilt.

AMOUNT OF MATERIAL

White ....7 yards
Light Blue ....1²/₃ yards
Dark Blue ....1²/₃ yards
Print ....1²/₃ yards

COLOR CHART

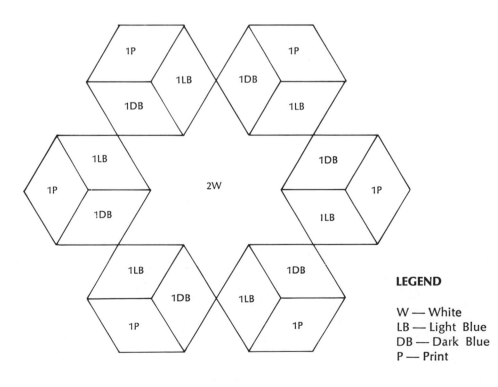

LEGEND

W — White
LB — Light Blue
DB — Dark Blue
P — Print

Patterns for this quilt are given on pages 37 and 39.

BOX QUILT

SIZE OF QUILT

This quilt, measuring 79½ x 88½ inches, is made up of seventy-two 9–inch pieced blocks set eight in width and nine in length with a 3¾–inch plain border.

NUMBER OF PIECES TO BE CUT

NOTE: Cut strips first to get full length without piecing.

Piece No. 1 . . . . 72 Red
Piece No. 2 . . . . 288 Blue
Piece No. 3 . . . . 288 White

2 strips, 4¼ x 80 inches . . . . Red
2 strips, 4¼ x 89 inches . . . . Red

AMOUNT OF MATERIAL

Red . . . . 4 yards
Blue . . . . 3 yards
White . . . . 2½ yards

COLOR CHART

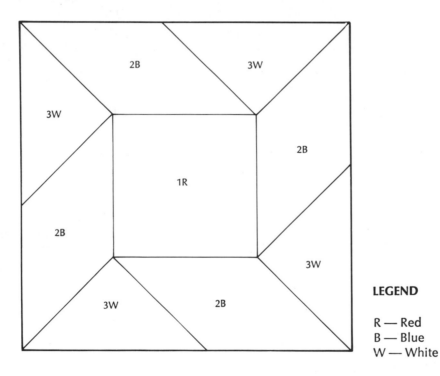

LEGEND

R — Red
B — Blue
W — White

Patterns for this quilt are given on page 41.

SUSPENSION BRIDGE QUILT

SIZE OF QUILT

This quilt, measuring 90 x 108 inches, is made up of twenty 18–inch pieced blocks set four in width and five in length with a 9–inch pieced scalloped border.

NUMBER OF PIECES TO BE CUT

Piece No. 1 . . . . 20 White
Piece No. 2 . . . . 98 Orange
Piece No. 3 . . . . .120 White
Piece No. 4 . . . . .720 White
Piece No. 5 . . . . .840 Orange
Piece No. 6 . . . . .240 White

AMOUNT OF MATERIAL

White . . . . .7½ yards
Orange . . . . .5½ yards

COLOR CHART

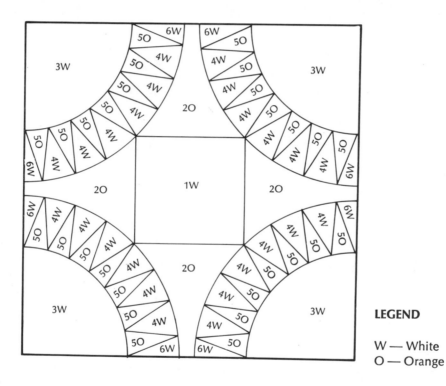

LEGEND

W — White
O — Orange

Patterns for this quilt are given on pages 43 and 45.

ROLLING STAR QUILT

SIZE OF QUILT

This quilt, measuring 75 x 90 inches, is made up of thirty 15-inch pieced blocks set five in width and six in length.

NUMBER OF PIECES TO BE CUT

Piece No. 1............360 Dark Green
Piece No. 1............120 Light Green
Piece No. 2............240 Print
Piece No. 3............120 White

AMOUNT OF MATERIAL

Dark Green ......4 yards
Light Green ......1⅓ yards
Print ....3⅓ yards
White ....2 yards

COLOR CHART

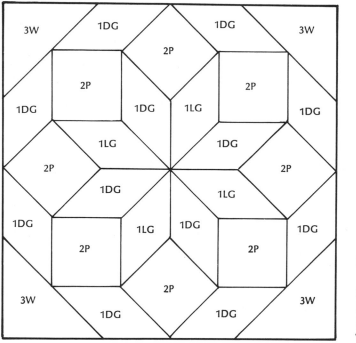

LEGEND

DG — Dark Green
LG — Light Green
P — Print
W — White

Patterns for this quilt are given on page 47.

SLASHED STAR QUILT

SIZE OF QUILT

This quilt, measuring 96 x 96 inches, is made up of sixteen 24–inch pieced blocks set four in width and four in length.

NUMBER OF PIECES TO BE CUT

Piece No. 1........ 64 White
Piece No. 2........192 Light Yellow
Piece No. 3........192 Medium Yellow
Piece No. 4........384 Dark Yellow
Piece No. 5........768 White
Piece No. 6........192 White
Piece No. 7........ 16 Red

AMOUNT OF MATERIAL

White ....9 yards
Medium Yellow ..2½ yards
Light Yellow .....2⅔ yards
Dark Yellow .....2⅓ yards
Red ....18 inches

COLOR CHART

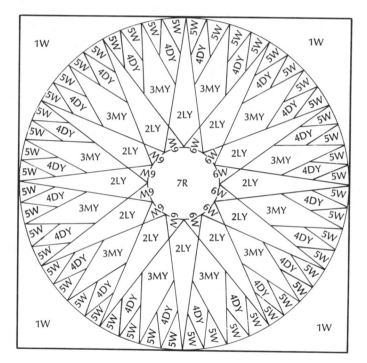

LEGEND

W — White
MY — Medium Yellow
LY — Light Yellow
DY — Dark Yellow
R — Red

Patterns for this quilt are given on pages 49 and 51.

STAR AND CUBES QUILT

SIZE OF QUILT

This quilt, measuring 80 x 98 inches, is made up of twenty 18–inch pieced blocks set four in width and five in length with a 4–inch plain border.

NUMBER OF PIECES TO BE CUT

NOTE: Cut strips first to get full length without piecing.

Piece No. 1 . . . . 80 White
Piece No. 2 . . . . 80 White
Piece No. 3 . . . . .160 Solid Color
Piece No. 4 . . . . .640 Print
Piece No. 5 . . . . .240 White

2 strips, 4½ x 80½ inches. . .Solid Color
2 strips, 4½ x 98½ inches. . .Solid Color

AMOUNT OF MATERIAL

White . . . . .4½ yards
Solid Color . . . . . .2⅔ yards
Print . . . . .2⅙ yards

COLOR CHART

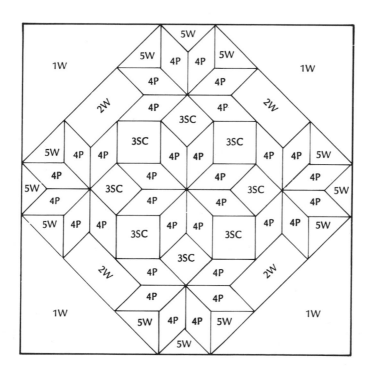

LEGEND

W — White
SC — Solid Color
P — Print

Patterns for this quilt are given on page 53.

GEORGETOWN CIRCLE QUILT

SIZE OF QUILT

This quilt, measuring 96 x 96 inches, is made up of nine 24–inch pieced blocks set three in width and three in length with four 3–inch plain border strips.

NUMBER OF PIECES TO BE CUT

NOTE: Cut strips first to get full length without piecing.

Piece No. 1 . . . . 72 Red
Piece No. 1 . . . . 72 Orange
Piece No. 2 . . . . 72 Red
Piece No. 2 . . . . 72 Yellow
Piece No. 3 . . . . 36 White
Piece No. 4 . . . . 288 White
Piece No. 5 . . . . 288 Orange
Piece No. 6 . . . . 72 White
Piece No. 7 . . . . 72 Red
Piece No. 8 . . . . 9 Orange

4 strips, 3½ x 78½ inches . . . . . . Red
4 strips, 3½ x 84½ inches . . . . . . Orange
4 strips, 3½ x 90½ inches . . . . . . Yellow
4 strips, 3½ x 96½ inches . . . . . . White

AMOUNT OF MATERIAL

Red . . . . .3¼ yards
Orange . . . . — 3¼ yards
Yellow . . . . — 2¼ yards
White . . . . 6¼ yards

COLOR CHART

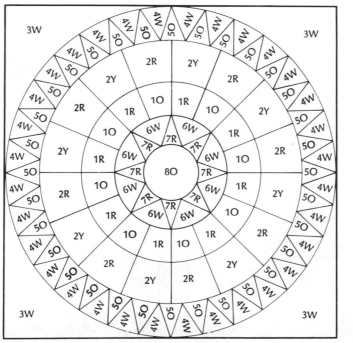

LEGEND

R — Red
O — Orange
Y — Yellow
W — White

Patterns for this quilt are given on pages 55 and 57.

CRAZY QUILT

SIZE OF QUILT

This quilt, measuring 78 x 96 inches, is made up of twenty 18–inch pieced blocks set four in width and five in length with a 3–inch plain border.

NUMBER OF PIECES TO BE CUT

NOTE: Cut strips first to get full length without piecing.

Piece No. 1........ 80 Solid Color
Piece No. 1a.......160 Solid Color
Piece No. 2.......320 Assorted Scraps*

2 strips, 3½ x 78½ inches...Solid Color
2 strips, 3½ x 96½ inches...Solid Color

*Piece No. 2 is cut from fabric which is prepared by sewing together small scraps of various materials.

AMOUNT OF MATERIAL

Solid Color .... 4 yards
Assorted Scraps ..1½ pounds

COLOR CHART

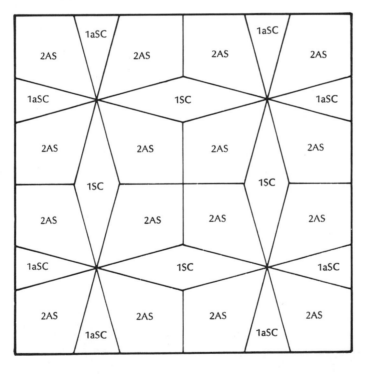

LEGEND

AS — Assorted Scraps
SC — Solid Color

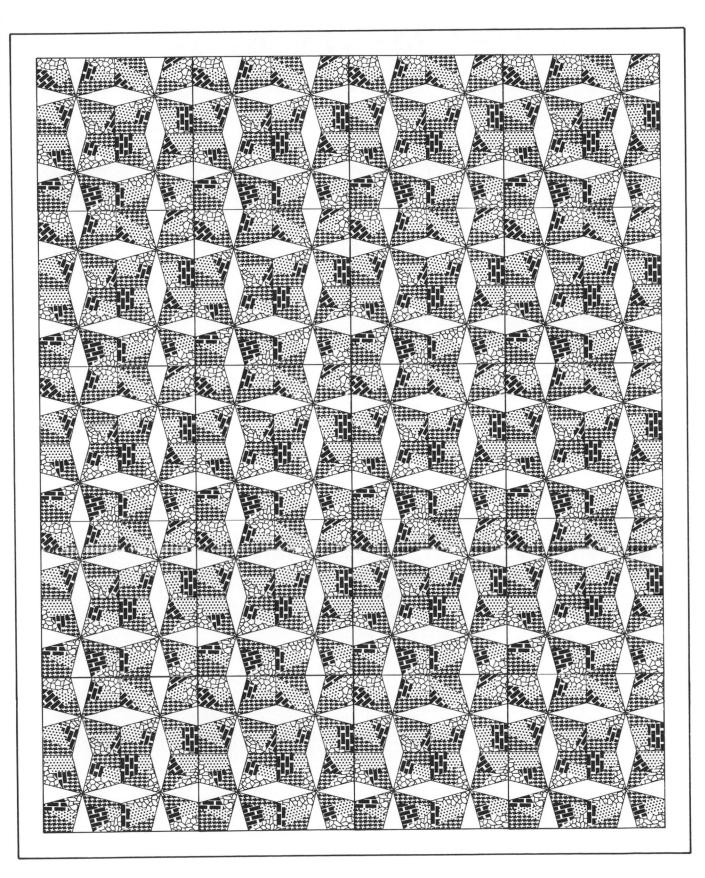

Patterns for this quilt are given on page 59.

SOLOMON'S TEMPLE QUILT

SIZE OF QUILT

This quilt, measuring 80 x 96 inches, is made up of an 8–inch pieced center square surrounded by nine 4–inch pieced square borders, with two additional border strips added at the top and bottom of the quilt to achieve the required length. The first border, which fits around the central 8–inch square, is made up of four pieced triangles and four No. 7 white triangles that form the corners of the square. The second border is made up of eight pieced triangles, four No. 6 triangles and four No. 7 triangles. The third border is made up of twelve pieced triangles, eight No. 6 triangles and four No. 7 triangles. The ninth border is made up of thirty-six pieced triangles, thirty-two No. 6 triangles and four No. 7 triangles. The four border strips added two at the top and two at the bottom to achieve the length are each made up of ten pieced triangles, nine No. 6 triangles and two No. 6a half-triangles used at each end of the border strip.

NUMBER OF PIECES TO BE CUT

Piece No. 1 . . . . 1 Red
Piece No. 2 . . . . .1772 Red
Piece No. 2 . . . . .1332 White
Piece No. 3 . . . . 222 White
Piece No. 3 . . . . 2 Red
Piece No. 4 . . . . 220 Red
Piece No. 5 . . . . 4 White
Piece No. 6 . . . . 180 White
Piece No. 6a . . . . 8 White*
Piece No. 7 . . . . 36 White

*Piece No. 6a is used *only* at the ends of the last two rows top and bottom.

AMOUNT OF MATERIAL

Red . . . . .5⅓ yards
White . . . . .6⅓ yards

COLOR CHART

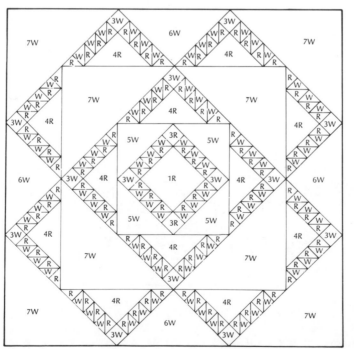

This piece, unnumbered in the color chart at left, is Piece No. 2.

LEGEND

R — Red
W — White

Patterns for this quilt are given on pages 61 and 63.